D.E.T.O.X.
DETOXING YOUR LIFE IN
5 FACETS TO FIND YOUR PURPOSE

*A Journey of Spiritual, Mental,
Physical, Financial, and Social Healing to
Rediscover Your True Self*

HARRY JEAN-SIMON

D.E.T.O.X.: Detoxing Your Life in 5 Facets To Find Your Purpose

Copyright © 2025 by Harry Jean-Simon

Purpose Publishing
13194 US Highway 301 S #417
Riverview, FL 33578
http://www.PurposePublishing.com

ISBN: 978-1-965319-44-4

All rights reserved. No part of this publication may be reproduced, distributed, or transmitted in any form or by any means, including photocopying, recording, or other electronic or mechanical methods, without the prior written permission of the publisher, except in the case of brief quotations embodied in critical reviews and certain other noncommercial uses permitted by copyright law. Printed in the United States of America.

TABLE OF CONTENTS

Introduction v

Foundational Scripture vii

Chapter 1: Spiritual D.E.T.O.X.—Breaking the Curse 1

Chapter 2: Mental D.E.T.O.X.—Reclaiming My Mind 7

Chapter 3: Physical D.E.T.O.X.—Rebuilding the Temple 13

Chapter 4: Financial D.E.T.O.X.—Breaking the Cycle, Building
    the Future 23

Chapter 5: Social D.E.T.O.X.—Reclaiming Your Circle,
    Rebuilding Your Environment 31

Chapter 6: The Finished Product 37

Chapter 7: It's Never Too Late 45

Chapter 8: It's Never Too Early to Teach the Legacy 53

Chapter 9: Me Versus Me 61

Chapter 10: Plain Sight—The Power of Positive Words 69

Chapter 11: The Lost Leading the Lost 85

Chapter 12: A World of Purposeful People 93

Conclusion 101

Biography 105

INTRODUCTION

D.E.T.O.X.
—A JOURNEY BACK TO YOU

D.E.T.O.X. is a blueprint for personal breakthrough. **D** stands for *Declutter*—removing what no longer serves you. **E** is for *Elevate*—rising to a higher standard mentally, spiritually, and emotionally. **T** means *Transform*—shifting your mindset and lifestyle from the inside out. **O** is for *Organize*—bringing order to your priorities, finances, and environment. And **X** is for *eXperience*—fully living and walking in the results of your growth. This process will be a complete life reset.

We live in a world that constantly pulls us in a thousand directions—some loud, some quiet, but all demanding a piece of us. Over time, without realizing it, we drift away from our true selves, acting as if we are someone else. We accumulate habits, relationships, mindsets, and lifestyles that no longer serve us. We become weighed down: spiritually, mentally, physically, financially, and socially.

This book is my journey of shedding that weight.

D.E.T.O.X. isn't just about green juices, supplements, and yoga mats. It's about releasing the toxic beliefs, people, systems, and behaviors that keep us stuck and small. It's about returning to your power and rediscovering your purpose. It's about making room for growth, healing, and transformation.

I know this path because I've walked it and am currently walking it every day—from the chaos of my childhood to the clarity I now carry as a man, a chef, an entrepreneur, and a human being who is dedicated to evolving. I've made mistakes. I've learned the lessons. Now, I'm here to share what I've discovered in five powerful stages that mirror the five key areas of our lives we must clean up to live freely and fully.

This is your invitation to take the mask off, look in the mirror, and say, "*I'm ready.*" Let's detox.

Harry Jean Simon

FOUNDATIONAL SCRIPTURE

*"And they overcame him by the blood of the Lamb,
and by the word of their testimony;
and they loved not their lives unto death."*

—Revelation 12:11 (KJV)

This scripture didn't end up in this book by accident—it found me.

My pastor, *Smokie Norful*, gave it to me during a powerful conversation that felt more like divine alignment than a meeting. He asked me a question I hadn't considered: **"What scripture will be the foundation of this message you're building?"**

I paused. I didn't have an answer at that moment, but what came next floored me. He said something that has always stuck with me: "This is bigger than a book. I see this as a film, a series, a movement." Then, he handed me Revelation 12:11.

It was confirmation. God had placed something inside me, and this scripture became the final seal. Not just a verse on a page—but a word that carried the weight of my story and the power of my purpose.

Still, I didn't take his word alone: I went home. I sat with it. I read it. Again. Then again. I asked God to speak through it, and He did.

I discovered that this scripture wasn't just about triumph. It was about transparency. It was about telling your truth—not just quietly surviving the pain but boldly proclaiming it, naming it, and facing it.

"They were overcome by the blood of the Lamb and by the word of their testimony …" That part hit me the hardest.

This book—this entire D.E.T.O.X. Journey—is built on that exact principle: Not hiding. Not shrinking. Not pretending but standing tall and saying, **"This is what I went through. This is what I faced. And by the grace of God, this is how I overcame it."**

This scripture became the spark that lit the flame of this detox: Spiritually, it called me into repentance and realignment. Mentally, it demanded I confront my thoughts and beliefs. Physically, it pushed me toward discipline and care for the vessel I've been given. Financially, it challenged my stewardship and self-worth. Socially, it revealed to me who I truly was by highlighting what I needed to release.

Revelation 12:11 isn't just a verse tucked into a page of this book—it's the **root**. It's the **reason** I began this journey. It's the **reminder** that everything I endured has power, purpose, and value when shared in truth and love.

So no, this isn't just a book. **It's a testimony**, and testimony is how we overcome it.

CHAPTER 1

SPIRITUAL D.E.T.O.X. —BREAKING THE CURSE

"Create in me a clean heart, O God; and renew a right spirit within me."

—Psalm 51:10

There comes a moment in every man's life where he must choose: carry the pain or confront it. Keep the silence or break the curse. That moment came for me not in a church pew or during a peaceful meditation but in the middle of a storm.

As a Haitian-American boy growing up on the South Side of Chicago, I was raised in the Catholic Church. I went to Catholic school, wore the uniform, memorized the prayers, and played my part. My mother believed in it deeply, and when you're a child, your mother's faith becomes your own by default. Yet even then, I felt a quiet disconnection. Something in me knew that this version of God was too small, too boxed in. The rituals were rich in tradition, but something was missing—the *relationship*.

It took years for me to realize I wasn't losing my religion—I was finding my spirituality. I wasn't turning my back on God. I was walking toward Him, finally on my own two feet.

Becoming nondenominational was the beginning of my reclaiming my faith. My mother would not have agreed with that decision. For her, it would've been like I was walking away from everything sacred. However, for me, it was a matter of walking toward the truth. My truth. I didn't stop reading the Bible. I didn't stop believing. I learned to stop pretending that rituals alone could heal what was broken inside me.

Yet nothing would test that new faith more than what I was forced to confront later in life. The deepest wound I've ever endured came from someone who shared my blood, my name, and even my birthday: my father, a man who not only failed to love me but succeeded in wounding nearly everyone connected to him. I found myself in the same unconscious situation.

I remember the moment I found out. A family member—someone I love and protect with every piece of me—confided in me about something she had carried since childhood. At just five or six years old, my father had molested her. She didn't tell me until she was twenty-five.

Think about that. That's almost two decades of silent pain. Two decades of trying to make sense of something senseless. Her voice shook, but her truth was solid, and when I heard it, I felt something break inside me.

Anger doesn't even begin to describe it. Rage came first. Then sorrow. Then, a type of clarity I can't explain. I got in my car and drove straight to his house—not out of confusion, but with purpose. I knew exactly what I was going to do. I decided I had two options: call the police or handle it myself. One way or another, justice would meet him at his doorstep. I brought her with me—the one he hurt—because she deserved to be seen and heard. She deserved to watch the man who broke her innocence be held accountable: her own grandfather.

He opened the door, and for the first time in my life, I wasn't afraid of him. I wasn't the little boy he used to talk down to. I was a man, a protector, and I had something to say—not just for her, but for all eleven of us: my siblings, each with our own pain. Each with a story of abuse—physical, emotional, or both. I let him have every word, and I held nothing back. My last words to him were, "Go kill yourself!"

He tried to deny it until I brought her in to confront him. He didn't apologize either. He just stood there: small, pitiful, silent. He looked up into my eyes like I looked at him when I was a boy— terrified.

That's when it hit me. He had been carrying demons for decades. He wasn't just a bad father. He was a broken man. He didn't just hurt us—he had never been whole himself. That doesn't excuse him, but it explains the generational sickness. Trauma is a torch passed down in silence, and until someone throws it into the fire, it continues to burn.

A week later, he died of cancer. It was Mother's Day. I'll never forget it.

He never made peace. Never righted his wrongs. Never asked for forgiveness. But I did something he never could—I vowed to confront the pain, not become it. I chose to detox my spirit.

My spiritual detox started long before that day, but it deepened afterward. I began rising early—not just to grind, but to *listen*. I'd start my mornings in prayer. Not the robotic, memorized ones from my Catholic childhood, but honest conversations with God. Then, I'd sit in stillness and meditate. That's where I learned to listen. That's where I learned to release.

Meditation helped me clean house. Prayer helped me rebuild it.

For so long, I didn't know how to pray. My prayers were surface-level, more traditional than transformational. Meditation taught me how to block out the noise, center my mind on God, and dig beneath the surface to the parts of me that most needed healing.

This is what I discovered: Healing is holy. Stillness is sacred, and you don't have to carry the weight of what was done to you. You couldn't do it by yourself even if you tried.

That's what spiritual detox is about. It's not just about letting go of what others did to you. It's about letting go of what you believe because of it. I believed I wasn't good enough. I believed I wasn't lovable. I believed I was alone. Yet none of that was ever true. I just had to dig through the lies to find God's truth again.

I made a vow that the curses would stop with me. I'm raising my children differently. I'm living differently. I'm choosing to be whole, even if it means doing the work no one before me was willing to do.

So here I stand—cleaner, sharper, freer. Is freer a word?

Therefore, *D.E.T.O.X.* begins here. The spirit must be grounded before the mind can be renewed. So I planted my feet in faith, released what wasn't mine to carry, and began to rebuild—not just for me but for every generation after me.

This was my spiritual detox and the foundation for everything that followed.

Spiritual D.E.T.O.X. Reflections
Daily Practices to Renew Your Spirituality

Spiritual detox begins with awareness—recognizing what has come between you and your Creator. In Chapter 1, you revisited your foundations: your upbringing, your values, and your earliest spiritual exposures. Now, it's time to begin renewing your spirit with simple, intentional daily habits.

These practices are designed to help you reconnect, realign, and refocus spiritually—no matter where you're starting from.

1. Morning Alignment Prayer

Start each day with this centering prayer:

> *"God, I surrender my thoughts, my plans, and my will to You. Cleanse my spirit of anything that doesn't reflect You. Fill me with peace, purpose, and power to walk in alignment with You today."*

Optional: Add your own prayer, personalized for your current season.

2. Scripture Meditation (5 minutes)

Choose one scripture each morning and sit with it for a moment. Read it slowly. Write it down. Let it speak to you.

> Suggested Verse: "Create in me a clean heart, O God, and renew a right spirit within me."—Psalm 51:10

Ask: *What is this scripture asking me to let go of or embrace today?*

3. Spiritual Journal Prompt

At the end of each day, respond to:

> *"Where did I feel closest to God today? Where did I feel far from Him?"*

Be honest. Your spiritual detox begins with reflection, not perfection.

4. Common Distractions

Pick one spiritual toxin to release for the day: social media, gossip, overthinking, negative music, comparison, etc.

> *D.E.T.O.X. Tip:* Replace it with worship, silence, scripture reading, or a walk with God.

5. Speak Spiritual Life

Affirm your spirit with daily declarations:

- *"The Spirit of God leads me."*

- *"I am enough because He is more than enough."*

- *"Today I walk in faith, not fear."*

Write one on a sticky note. Post it near your mirror, dashboard, or phone screen.

6. Evening Surrender

End the day with stillness. Breathe deeply and say:

> *"God, I release today. Cleanse my spirit from anything that grieved You. Thank You for staying close, even when I drifted. Tomorrow, I walk with fresh grace."*

Closing Reminder

You don't have to be perfect to be present. God doesn't expect performance—He desires connection. Each small spiritual habit opens the door for renewal. Let this chapter mark the beginning of your daily return to the Source.

CHAPTER 2

MENTAL D.E.T.O.X. —RECLAIMING MY MIND

"Do not conform to the pattern of this world, but be transformed by the renewing of your mind."

—Romans 12:2

Before I could truly change my life and heart, I had to change my mind.

After the spiritual detox, I felt lighter in my soul, but my thoughts were still heavy. Even with a clearer connection to God, I was still mentally fighting ghosts from the past: fear, doubt,

shame, and most of all, the echo of my father's voice that told me I'd never be anything.

That voice lingered longer than I realized. It shaped how I saw myself, how I talked to myself, how I moved in rooms—even when I was more than qualified to be there. It made me question my worth. My value. My future.

It's crazy how someone else's brokenness can become the background noise in your mind if you never learn to silence it.

I had to take a hard look at my thoughts: where they came from, who planted them, and whether they still served me. That's when I realized my mind was overcrowded with ideas, identities, and insecurities that weren't even mine.

See, mental detox is about clearing space—space to think without distraction, dream freely, and, most importantly, believe in yourself. It's about stripping away the mental clutter of everything that's been projected onto you. It's about replacing negative loops with intentional truth.

I grew up in survival mode, which teaches you to think small, move carefully, and expect the worst because you've seen too much of it. But healing taught me something different: your mind is your engine, and what you feed it fuels your life.

When I started to meditate, it wasn't just about finding peace—it was about hearing myself again. Not the me that was traumatized, but the me that was powerful. The me that still had a vision. The me that God made before the world tried to label me.

I realized how many years I spent operating from fear:

- Fear of failing
- Fear of success
- Fear of disappointing people
- Fear of becoming my father
- Fear of not becoming enough

However, mental detox helped me start challenging those thoughts. Just because a thought shows up doesn't mean it belongs. Just because a belief was handed to me doesn't mean I must accept it.

I had to reprogram my mind the same way I detoxed my spirit—daily. I began to replace every limiting thought with something rooted in truth:

I am not my past.

I am not what they said about me.

I am not the worst thing I've experienced.

I am worthy of peace, success, and love.

I am chosen and capable, right now, as I am.

So when those old thoughts tried to creep back, I stopped letting them move in. They could knock, but they couldn't stay.

I also realized how powerful silence is. Sometimes, we're afraid to sit in silence because it's then that the most profound thoughts surface. However, silence is where the healing begins. It's where you meet yourself without the noise. Most importantly, it's where you can hear God whisper truth over your life.

Mental detox doesn't mean your mind will never struggle again—it means you've built the tools to fight back. You no longer surrender to every negative spiral. You pause. You breathe. You realign. This stage taught me how to protect my peace and train my thoughts to serve me—not sabotage me. Because once your mind is free, everything else begins to shift. That's when vision returns. That's when clarity comes. That's when your purpose starts speaking louder than your pain.

Mental D.E.T.O.X. Reflections
Daily Practices to Renew Your Mentality

The mind is where battles are won—or lost. In Chapter 2, you explored what it means to detox spiritually. Yet without mental renewal, even the strongest spiritual intentions can be clouded by doubt, anxiety, or distraction.

These daily mental detox practices are designed to cleanse your thoughts, focus your energy, and realign your mindset with the life God intended for you.

1. Daily Thought Check

Begin each day by writing down the first three thoughts that come to mind. Then ask yourself:

Are these thoughts rooted in faith, fear, or frustration?

If they are not serving your growth, rewrite each one with truth and purpose.

2. Affirm the Shift

Choose one of the following mental affirmations each day—or create your own:

- *"I release what I cannot control and focus on what I can."*

- *"My thoughts are disciplined, powerful, and aligned with peace."*

- *"I take every thought captive and make it obedient to Christ."*—2 Corinthians 10:5

Speak it out loud. Say it with intention.

3. Clarity Moment (Midday Reset)

Pause in the middle of your day. Find a quiet space for three to five minutes. Close your eyes and ask:

"Where is my mind right now? Am I present or distracted? Aligned or anxious?"

Take five deep breaths. Release tension. Invite clarity. Let go of what's not yours to carry.

4. Limit the Noise

Choose one thing to *mute* or *minimize* daily: negative news, unnecessary scrolling, gossip, overcommitted schedules, or toxic conversations.

Replace that space with:

- A podcast that feeds your spirit

- A devotional or uplifting reading

- Moments of complete silence

5. Evening Mind Dump

Before bed, write down every lingering thought in your mind—no filter: worries, ideas, to-dos, feelings.

Then close your journal and pray:

> *"God, I give You my thoughts tonight. Clear the clutter, restore my peace, and renew my mind."*

6. Weekly Mental Audit

Once a week, reflect on:

- What triggered you mentally this week?

- What repeated thought kept showing up?

- What boundaries do you need to protect your peace?

Awareness is the first step to transformation.

Closing Reminder

A renewed mentality doesn't just think differently—it sees life differently. Detoxing your mind daily enables you to hear God more clearly, respond to challenges with grace, and stay anchored in your purpose. Protect your peace. Guard your thoughts. Your mind is sacred ground.

CHAPTER 3

PHYSICAL D.E.T.O.X. —REBUILDING THE TEMPLE

"Do you not know that your bodies are temples of the Holy Spirit, who is in you, whom you have received from God? You are not your own."

—1 Corinthians 6:19

Growing up, I never gave much thought to what I ate. I had one of those metabolisms that burned off everything. I mean everything. I could eat five beef patties, a plate of diri ak djon djon (black mushroom rice), fried plantains, and wash it all down with a tall glass of Kool-Aid and still have room for dessert—and I wouldn't gain a pound. Back then, my body felt invincible. I was always moving—playing sports, racing neighborhood kids, jumping fences, doing backflips in the grass.

I wanted to be an athlete, not just for the love of the game but for the brotherhood. That sense of team, connection, and pushing each other to be better lit something up inside me. Now, fast forward to adulthood. That fast metabolism? Gone. The stress? High. The activity level? Inconsistent. The eating habits? Slipping. I was still moving, working, and grinding, but my body began to whisper to me. Then those whispers turned into warnings.

The Wake-Up Call: Blood Pressure and Breaking the Pattern

It all hit me during what I thought would be a routine checkup. I remember sitting in that chair, the cuff tightening on my arm, not expecting anything unusual. Then the nurse looked at me, concern written all over her face.

"Your blood pressure is 198 over 124."

I froze. That wasn't just high—that was *stroke-level* high. I'm a chef, for crying out loud. I know better. Yet the truth is that knowing and *doing* are two different things.

I realized that even though I cooked fresh and healthy meals for my clients and family, I wasn't doing the same for myself. I was grabbing food on the go, eating out more than I should, and ignoring the salt, sugar, and preservatives that sneak into nearly everything served at restaurants. Mix that with stress, little sleep, and not enough movement, and it's no wonder my body finally screamed.

That moment forced me to confront the truth: I had to detox physically, just like I had been doing spiritually and mentally. My temple needed rebuilding.

The Clean-Out: Liquid and Gut Reset

Before you start feeding your body with all the good stuff, you've got to clean out the mess. You wouldn't pour clean water into a dirty cup and call it pure, right? So I started with the foundation: my gut. I committed to a six-to-seven-day liquid detox. It wasn't easy—believe me—but it changed everything. Here's what I did:

- **Liquids only:** Fresh juices, herbal teas, healing broths, and nutrient-rich smoothies

- **Probiotics daily:** To rebuild my gut with good bacteria

- **A gallon of water every day:** To flush out toxins

- **Prayer and meditation:** Aligned my spirit with my healing process every morning

During this detox, I felt a shift—not just physically but mentally. I was clearer. More grounded. My cravings disappeared. Then the proof came: my blood pressure dropped from 198/124 to 117/79.

That's not just a health stat—that's a testimony. That's God reminding me that when you give your body what it needs, it responds with life.

The Rebuild: Movement and Fuel

After the cleanse, I didn't stop. I kept going, rebuilding the right way. I became intentional with everything I put in my body.

- **High-protein meals** to repair

- **Greens and superfoods** to energize

- **Herbs and spices** instead of salt

- **Homemade Haitian dishes**—Yes! The same ones I grew up on, but now with a twist. I learned how to cook my favorites like legim, tassot, and lalo using healthier oils, less sodium, and more vegetables. I didn't lose the flavor—I just gained the benefits.

Cooking this way became healing. It was like honoring my roots *and* my health simultaneously. The food still spoke to my soul, but it stopped hurting my body.

I moved daily. Some days, it was the gym. On other days, it was a walk or a stretching session. I listened to my body: I rested when I needed to, slept more, recovered more, and ate with intention. I became my own trainer, my own nutritionist, and my own healer.

The Truth About the Plate

Here's what I've learned the hard way: **what's on your plate can either be your medicine or your poison.**

Every bite is a choice. When you always eat out, you give up control over those choices. You don't know how much salt they used. You don't know what kind of oil is in that pan. You don't know if that meat was pumped with hormones. You're just trusting strangers with your temple—and that's risky.

So now, I choose to cook. Not just because I'm a chef, but because I care about what I put into this vessel God gave me. I encourage you to do the same—start with just one meal. One clean plate. Learn what your body needs, then give it that love daily.

Physical D.E.T.O.X. Reflections
Daily Practices to Renew Your Temple (Your Body)

Your body is not just a vessel—it's your temple. It carries your spirit, fuels your purpose, and reflects how well you honor what God has given you. In Chapter 3, you were challenged to detox your physical life by becoming more intentional about what you consume, how you move, and how you treat your body.

These daily practices will help you restore energy, discipline, and balance while aligning your physical health with your spiritual calling.

1. Morning Body Check-In

Upon waking, take two minutes before grabbing your phone or starting your day. Ask yourself:

> *"How does my body feel this morning? What does it need—movement, water, rest, nourishment?"*

Write down or say one small commitment for your body today:

- *"I will drink more water."*

- *"I will stretch and breathe."*

- *"I will nourish myself, not punish myself."*

2. Fuel with Intention

Each meal is an opportunity to heal or harm. Ask:

"Is this food fueling my purpose or feeding my cravings?"

Start simple:

- Drink at least half your body weight in ounces of water.

- Add more living foods, such as fruits, vegetables, and herbs.

- Reduce processed foods, added sugars, and chemical-laden snacks.

Reminder: You don't have to change everything overnight—start with one better choice each day.

3. Move with Gratitude (15–30 minutes)

Your body was made to move—not just for fitness, but for freedom.

Choose a type of movement you enjoy:

- Walking while praying or reflecting

- Stretching while listening to worship

- Dancing, biking, light workouts, or deep breathing

As you move, say:

"Thank You, God, for a body that still works, heals, and responds to love."

4. Rest and Recovery

D.E.T.O.X. includes *what you stop doing,* too. Your body needs stillness and restoration.

Ask:

"Am I getting enough sleep, or am I surviving on fumes?"

Daily rest detox practices:

- Shut off screens 30–60 minutes before bed.

- Take a power nap if needed during the day.

- Practice "Sabbath rest" weekly—physically and mentally unplug.

5. Body Affirmation

Look in the mirror daily and declare:

- *"My body is a gift from God. I care for it with love, not shame."*

- *"I honor my temple with rest, movement, and nourishment."*

- *"I'm not chasing perfection—I'm committing to progress."*

6. Weekly D.E.T.O.X. Reset

Once a week, evaluate:

- Did I treat my body with respect this week?

- What made me feel energized or drained?

- What slight shift can I make this week to support my physical wellness?

Celebrate your wins—no matter how small.

Closing Reminder

Your body is a divine instrument. Not perfect, but purposeful. Not flawless, but favored. A transformative physical detox is not about weight loss—it's about alignment, stewardship, and love. When your temple is cared for, you can carry your purpose with power.

> **You don't have to be perfect—you only have to be present.**
> Start fresh. Reset. D.E.T.O.X.. Rise again, stronger.

CHAPTER 4

FINANCIAL D.E.T.O.X.—BREAKING THE CYCLE, BUILDING THE FUTURE

"The borrower is slave to the lender."

—Proverbs 22:7

Let me keep it real with you.

There was a time when money had a chokehold on me—not just on my wallet but on my *mind*, my *habits*, my *self-worth*, and my *future*. I wasn't broke on paper, but I was spiritually and mentally bankrupt when it came to how I managed money. I was bound: Bound by bad habits. Bound by fear. Bound by a lack of knowledge passed down for generations.

Realistically, financial detoxing isn't just about saving a couple of dollars or getting out of debt. It's about going deep to unlearn the patterns you picked up from your environment, your community, and even your family. It's about acknowledging the cycles handed to us—not out of malice, but out of survival.

From Hustle to Healing: What I Saw Growing Up

Growing up, I saw my mother grind hard. She was a warrior. She did what she could to keep food on the table and a roof over our heads. I'll always love her for that, but looking back, I realize this: she worked *hard*, not *smart*. Not because she didn't want to be smarter with money, but because no one ever taught her how.

Financial literacy wasn't a subject in the school where I came from. We didn't have classes on credit, taxes, budgeting, or passive income. Nah, we learned about money by watching people *react* to it: stressing out over bills, celebrating on payday, and going back to broke by Monday.

I also saw another side of the game: the streets. I watched drug dealers chase fast money, blow it even faster, and live with no exit plan. I saw dudes wearing designer clothes, popping bottles, and flexing, but they had no assets, retirement, savings, or insurance. Yet somehow, that lifestyle looked more attractive than a 9-to-5.

So I followed what I saw.

I grew up thinking credit was something to *avoid*, not *build*. I thought success was about what you wore, what you drove, and how many people knew your name. I picked up bad habits, such as swiping cards I couldn't pay off, living off refunds, maxing out limits, and ignoring bills until they turned red.

Boy, when I started doing research later in life, I realized *I had it all wrong*.

My Financial Reality Check: From Drowning to D.E.T.O.X.

Before BreakinBread21 became a business, I was juggling jobs. I always brought value wherever I worked. I was the guy everyone loved, the one people looked to for leadership and excellent service. However, being the "face" of a company didn't mean I was being *paid* like one.

I was overworked, underpaid, and one emergency away from collapse. There were nights I went to bed anxious, knowing I couldn't cover a bill, pay a fine, or help my kids how I wanted to. Has your child ever called for help with something you *know* they deserve, but you couldn't provide it? That cuts deep. That doesn't just hurt your pockets—it hurts your *pride* as a man.

At one point, I was nearly $70,000 in debt: credit cards, loans, and subscriptions I'd forgotten to cancel. I had a beautiful truck on the outside, but the dashboard lit up like a Christmas tree, and I didn't have the money to fix it.

I was trying to invest in myself, but it felt like I was playing from behind. Like I was sprinting through mud. I was hustling, but I had no strategy.

That's when I said, "*Enough is enough.*"

The D.E.T.O.X. Begins: Calling It What It Is

I started my financial detox with one word: *truth*.

I had to admit I was financially toxic. I couldn't keep asking God to bless me with more if I was mismanaging the little I had. Just like your body can't absorb nutrients when your system is backed up, your life can't receive wealth when debt, bad habits, and emotional spending weigh you down.

So here's what I did:

- I pulled up my bank statements and read them like a diary.

- I tracked every dollar and gave it an assignment.

- I deleted apps that made it too easy to spend.

- I stopped spending based on feelings and started spending based on facts.

- I faced the complete list of what I owed and didn't run from it this time.

- Most importantly, I forgave myself.

This is why. Please hear this: Shame doesn't build wealth. Discipline does.

The Rebuild: Learning the Language of Wealth

I became a student again. I picked up books such as *Rich Dad Poor Dad*, *Think and Grow Rich*, *The Psychology of Money*, *MONEY: Master the Game*, and *Full-Time CEO*.

I stopped treating my business like a hustle and started treating it like a company. I separated my business account from my personal one. I learned how to price my services right. I started saving for taxes instead of being surprised by them. I started thinking like a CEO, not a laborer.

I also learned how money actually works. Credit isn't bad—it's a tool if you use it correctly. Budgeting isn't restrictive—it's liberating. Building wealth doesn't come from flashy income—it comes from quiet discipline.

From Survival Mode to Freedom Living

This journey ain't about being perfect. It's about being intentional. I'm not trying to impress anybody anymore—I'm trying to leave a legacy.

I'm not just living paycheck to paycheck—I'm building a foundation my kids and grandkids can stand on.

That's what financial detoxing is really about.

It's not about how much money you make. It's about what you keep, what you invest, and how you *manage* what you have—faithfully, wisely, and consistently.

Financial D.E.T.O.X. Reflections
Daily Practices to Renew Your Mindset About Money

Money is not just a resource—it's a reflection of mindset, discipline, and spiritual stewardship. In Chapter 4, you were invited to detox your financial life by challenging old money habits, breaking generational patterns, and developing a healthier relationship with wealth.

These daily practices will help you rewire your thoughts about money, take intentional action, and align your finances with your values and vision.

1. Daily Money Mindset Check

Each morning, ask yourself:

> *"What is my dominant belief about money today—fear, frustration, faith, or focus?"*

Then declare:

- *"I have more than enough to meet every need."*

- *"I attract wise opportunities and steward them well."*

- *"Money flows to me because I'm aligned with purpose."*

2. Track One Transaction

D.E.T.O.X. starts with awareness. Write down just **one transaction** per day. Ask:

> *"Was this a wise investment, an emotional expense, or a necessary purchase?"*

Over time, this habit will reveal your patterns—and help you make better decisions.

3. 10-Minute Financial Review

Set aside 10 minutes daily to:

- Check your bank balance without fear.

- Pay down a small debt or round up a payment.

- Move $5–$25 into a savings or emergency account.

Taking small steps daily can build unstoppable momentum financially.

4. Speak Prosperity, Not Poverty

Replace limiting language like:

- "I'm broke."

- "I can't afford that."

- "I'll never get out of debt."

With:

- "I'm learning how to manage abundance."

- "I'm building wealth with wisdom."

- "I honor God and myself with every dollar I steward."

5. Weekly Financial D.E.T.O.X. Practice

Once a week, perform one of the following:

- Review and cancel unused subscriptions.

- Create or update your budget using the 80/10/10 method (Live/Save/Give).

- Identify and plan for a future income stream or side business idea.

6. Generosity Activation

Even during a detox, giving is powerful. Choose one small weekly act of kindness:

- Tip extra with intention.

- Pay for someone's coffee or lunch.

- Tithe or sow into someone's life or dream.

Giving opens the door to receiving—emotionally, spiritually, and financially.

Closing Reminder

Financial detox isn't just about numbers—it's about mindset. Freedom begins when you stop serving money and start commanding it with clarity, confidence, and faith. You don't have to be rich to live a rich life. Honor your finances today, and they will honor your future.

CHAPTER 5

SOCIAL D.E.T.O.X.—RECLAIMING YOUR CIRCLE, REBUILDING YOUR ENVIRONMENT

"Do not be misled: 'Bad company corrupts good character.'"

—1 Corinthians 15:33 (NIV)

Let me be open with you: growing up, I always felt like I was different. I never liked being part of a clique. While other kids were loyal to one crew, one block, or one corner, I was the one walking through the whole neighborhood, talking to everybody. From the jocks to the hustlers, the church kids to the wild ones—I connected with them all. It was natural for me. I didn't like division. That also meant I couldn't pick sides, even when some of my friends became enemies. That put me in awkward positions, but deep down, I knew I wasn't meant to be boxed in.

I felt most at home with my Haitian community. Even though we were in America, our homes were still deeply rooted in Haitian culture. Same values. Same rules. Same expectations. Same discipline! While that gave me strength and structure, it also created an underlying tension because the culture inside our homes didn't always line up with what was happening outside on the streets or at school.

See, in Haitian households, you grow up fast. You respect elders, stay sharp, and keep your mouth shut unless spoken to. But in American culture—especially in the hood—you gotta learn how to survive by speaking up, showing out, or blending in. So I was constantly navigating two worlds. Sometimes, I didn't feel like I fit in either.

I was a dreamer. Even as a kid, I saw something bigger. I didn't always know what it was or how to get there, but I knew I was created for more. The problem was that I didn't have the setup: No mentors. No financial literacy classes. No real guidance on how to turn dreams into plans. I thought opportunity was something rich kids got. I thought the bag was the only way out, so I chased it. Hard.

Looking back now, I see it so clearly. Opportunities were everywhere, but I didn't know how to recognize them. I didn't realize I was chasing the bag when I should've been chasing the truth. Because when you chase truth, the bag will always find its way to you.

Social D.E.T.O.X.: More Than Just Cutting People Off

Detoxing socially isn't just about dropping toxic people. It's about checking everything—your crew, your content, your conversations, your energy. What are you feeding your spirit? Who's feeding your mindset? What are you allowing in?

Growing up on the South Side of Chicago, my circle was full of raw, unfiltered love but also pain and trauma. The block taught us loyalty, but it also taught us to put up emotional armor. Some of my closest friends from back then? Gone too soon. Gun violence, drugs, jail. I lost too many to count. That kind of pain never truly fades, but it fueled me to live differently: to be intentional, protect my peace, and choose my people wisely. I realized a social detox wasn't just necessary—it was urgent.

We don't talk enough about how what we watch and listen to affects us just as much as who we hang with. Social media? Man, it's a beast. The scroll is slow poison if you're not careful. One minute, you're looking for inspiration. The next thing you know, you're comparing your real life to someone else's highlight reel. You start feeling behind, less than, unworthy—all from a screen.

So I started unfollowing people, muted the drama, and turned down the volume on the noise. I replaced all that junk with things that fed my mind: documentaries, deep podcasts, and interviews with leaders and visionaries. It changed how I thought and, eventually, how I moved. You can't grow in toxic soil. You can't level up in rooms full of envy and confusion.

Your circle is either sharpening you or shaving you down.

When Silence Was My Teacher

Let me tell you something else: support was rare, even inside my own home growing up. I wasn't getting "I'm proud of you" or "You got this." It was more like, "Why'd you do that?" "That's not good enough."

Don't get me wrong—I know my parents did their best with what they had. But that lack of affirmation? It sticks with a young man. You grow up always questioning yourself, wondering if you're enough. Then, you carry that into friendships, jobs, relationships, and even fatherhood.

As a man, I had to unlearn all of that. I had to learn to accept feedback without taking it personally and believe in myself even when no one else clapped. Most importantly, I had to learn how to create the environment I *needed* rather than just accepting the one I was given.

Peace Over Popularity

After being burned by a few business relationships and so-called friends, I started choosing peace over popularity. Some people only showed up when I was winning. When I lost? Crickets. That was my wake-up call.

I had to love some people from a distance. I had to say no—even when it was uncomfortable. Sometimes, the people who knew *the old you* can't handle the healed you. And yeah, it even meant pulling away from family sometimes.

I know that sounds harsh, but hear me: peace is expensive, but it's worth every penny.

Travel as Therapy

These days, traveling is an integral part of my healing. Whenever I step into a new city, try a new dish, or connect with someone different, I feel more alive. My wife and I travel often for our business, but it's deeper than just business—it's soul work. Experiencing new environments clears my head. It reminds me that the world is bigger than my pain, my past, or my neighborhood. Sometimes, all you need is a change of scenery to change your mindset.

Now, I Choose Differently

Now, I want to be a *healer* in every room I enter. I want people to feel lighter after talking to me—not heavier. I don't want to be the reason someone else needs a detox. That's what growth looks like. I protect my peace like it's my passport because I can't go anywhere worth going without it.

Social D.E.T.O.X. Reflections
Daily Practices to Protect Your Peace

These daily actions help detox your relationships and create space for more meaningful, purpose-driven connections.

1. Daily Circle Scan

Ask: *"Who did I interact with today, and how did it make me feel?"*

- Energized? Inspired? Grounded?

- Drained? Confused? Triggered?

Write down any patterns you notice over time.

2. Set One Boundary Today

Choose one small boundary to enforce—whether it's a delayed text reply, a "no" to an invitation, or pausing a conversation that crosses a line.

> *D.E.T.O.X. Tip:* Boundaries are not walls—they are doors with locks. You choose who gets access.

3. One Intentional Connection

Each day, text or call someone who adds value to your life. Be intentional:

- Send encouragement.

- Ask how they're really doing.

- Offer prayer, support, or gratitude.

4. Social Media Sweep

Unfollow, mute, or remove one account each day that no longer aligns with your mindset, goals, or values.

Less comparison, more clarity.

5. Speak Life in Your Circle

Start this habit:

- Compliment someone without conditions.

- Say, *"I appreciate you for ..."*

- Pray for someone silently or aloud.

Your energy is contagious. Detoxed people attract detoxed people.

Closing Reminder

Your environment influences your evolution. Detoxing socially isn't just about cutting people off—it's about cultivating the community you deserve. Who surrounds you will either stir your calling or stifle it. Choose wisely. Protect your peace. Love doesn't always mean access.

CHAPTER 6

THE FINISHED PRODUCT

"Being confident of this very thing, that He who has begun a good work in you will complete it until the day of Jesus Christ."

—Philippians 1:6

There's something sacred about **becoming**: Not arriving. Not being perfect. Not having it all figured out. Just ... becoming.

For a long time, I didn't even know what I was becoming. All I knew was that I was different.

Even as a kid, I saw the world through a different lens. While most people were surviving the day, I was dreaming about tomorrow—about building something, creating something, becoming *someone*. Only I didn't have the words for it back then.

From the Block to the Blueprint

Growing up in the neighborhoods I did, there weren't many people walking around talking about purpose or alignment. Nobody was giving out blueprints to build something of your own—at least not legally. The loudest voices were the ones telling you to "get yours," "watch your back," or "don't trust anybody." However, deep inside, I always felt like there was more.

I remember being that kid who asked too many questions. The one who couldn't sit still—not because I was bad, but because I was curious. I wanted to know why things were the way they were. Why did we struggle? Why did our parents work so hard and still have so little? Why did certain families have structure and peace while others were drowning in chaos? No matter what was happening around me, I always had this little voice inside saying, "You were built for more."

I flat-out didn't know how to get there, and to be honest with you? I didn't always believe I could, but life has a way of molding you if you let it. Pain became my professor. Mistakes became my mentors, and God? He never stopped working on me—even when I didn't see it.

The D.E.T.O.X. Was Just the Beginning

Detoxing wasn't about becoming someone else—it was about returning to who I authentically was all along. After the spiritual reset. After the mental stillness. After the physical discipline, the financial awareness, and the social alignment. I saw something in the mirror I hadn't seen in a long time: the *real* me.

The boy who once felt stuck now walks in freedom. The dreamer who felt out of place now creates spaces for others. The kid who once felt like he wasn't enough is building enough for future generations. This is what the *"finished product"* of my detox looks like:

I Am an Entrepreneur

I don't just sell food or ideas—I build visions. I'm not afraid to bet on myself anymore. Yes, I've failed, but failure taught me more than comfort ever could. I'm a student of life—a student of purpose. I study people, patterns, and God's whispers. My business isn't just about profit—it's about impact. It's about leaving fingerprints on the world.

I Am an Author

Every page I write is therapy for both me and the reader. This book isn't just a product—it's a piece of my soul. I took all the stories, trauma, and truth and turned them into something that can free someone else. That's legacy. That's the purpose in print.

I Am a Speaker

My voice carries something now. It's not just noise—it's assignment. I've spoken in kitchens, at family tables, on flights, and in front of strangers, and I know what I carry. I don't just speak to inspire. I speak to activate. God gave me this voice to heal rooms and unlock chains.

I Am a Chef

I am not just someone who cooks—I'm someone who connects. Food is my language. My art. My ministry. With BreakinBread21, I don't just serve meals—I serve memories, healing, and heritage. Every dish has a story. Every plate is an offering.

I Am a Host

Whether I'm throwing a dinner, leading a retreat, or just creating a safe space, people *feel* me. I create environments where people know they're seen, loved, and fed—body, mind, and soul.

Hospitality runs deep in my blood—in how I treat people. It's how I honor God.

I Am God's Son

Above every title—entrepreneur, chef, author—I am a child of the King. I don't walk in shame anymore. I walk in identity. I know who I am. I hear God more clearly now because I've removed the noise, and when He speaks, I listen.

I Live in Clarity

No more fog. No more faking it. I know where I'm going. I know who's with me. I know who I am without the applause.

I Am a Light

Wherever I go, I bring warmth. God kept my heart soft even when the world tried to harden me. The detox didn't just cleanse me—it uncovered me. I was always the light—I merely had to wipe off the dirt. Now I see it so clearly. Everything I walked through was never meant to break me—it was intended to *build* me. To give me grit. To develop my character. To prepare me for the lives I'm called to impact.

If You're Reading This …

You might be in the middle of your own detox right now. You might be wondering what your "finished product" could look like. Let me tell you something: it's already *in you*.

It's in the late-night tears. It's in the "No" that shaped you. It's in the moments nobody saw—but God did. It's under the pain, past the fear, beyond the generational patterns.

You are becoming.
Keep going.
Keep detoxing.
Keep listening.
Keep showing up.

Because when God is the builder, there is no such thing as unfinished.

CHAPTER 6 REFLECTION
The Finished Product–Becoming Who You Were Designed to Be

This is what the process was for: transformation. The "Finished Product" is not perfection—it's alignment. It's the version of you that finally matches what God had in mind all along. This chapter reminded you that every detoxed area—spiritual, mental, physical, financial, social, emotional—has brought you closer to your authentic self.

You are not the same person who started this journey. You've let go. You've realigned. You've returned to truth. Now, you stand as the reflection of grace, healing, and purpose.

Reflection Questions

1. What parts of me have changed the most since starting this D.E.T.O.X. Journey?

2. What am I no longer willing to carry into my next chapter of life?

3. In what ways do I feel more whole, more present, or more grounded?

4. Which area of detox was the hardest for me? Why?

5. What lies have I replaced with truth?

6. How do I now define peace, purpose, and success?

7. What evidence do I have that the detox is working in my life?

8. What legacy do I want to leave as the "finished product"?

The Finished Product
Daily Practices to Stay Aligned

Now that you've done the work, the focus shifts to maintenance—keeping your spirit clean, your mind sharp, and your life in alignment. Here are some simple yet powerful practices to keep the transformation alive.

1. Morning Mirror Moment

Stand in front of the mirror. Look into your eyes and say:

> *"I am the finished work of grace. I am healed, whole, and walking in alignment."*

Speak it until you believe it.

2. The Alignment Check (Daily)

Ask yourself before any big decision, commitment, or conversation:

> *"Does this reflect the healed version of me—or the old one?"*

Only choose what aligns.

3. D.E.T.O.X. Reminder Journal

Each day, write one sentence that begins with:

> "Today, I'm choosing _____ because I'm no longer _____."
> Example: *Today, I'm choosing rest because I'm no longer trying to prove my worth through burnout.*

4. Purpose Walks

Walk in silence or with worship music for 15–30 minutes each week. Reflect on where you've come from and where God is leading you.

Ask: *"Am I still on the path—or do I need to realign?"*

5. Legacy Check-In (Weekly)

Once a week, reflect or journal on:

> *"If someone followed my life this week, what would they believe about God, healing, and purpose?"*

Let your life continue to speak.

Closing Reminder

You are the finished product—not because you're flawless, but because you're faithful. You said yes to the process. You showed up for your own healing, and now, you are proof that transformation is possible. Never forget: Detoxing wasn't about becoming someone new—it was about becoming **you.**

CHAPTER 7

IT'S NEVER TOO LATE

"Where there is no vision, the people perish."

—Proverbs 29:18

Let me be blunt with you: if you're reading this chapter thinking your best days are behind you, let me stop you right there. That's a lie—a dangerous one. I know because I believed it for a long time.

I turned fifty years old on September 10, 2024. That milestone hit hard. Half a century. A full five decades of breath, brokenness, breakthrough, and becoming. I didn't throw a big party. I didn't post a bunch of selfies. I sat with it. I reflected on my life—the wins, the losses, the detours, the doors I walked through, and the ones I slammed shut.

I realized something powerful. I'm not at the end—I'm just getting started.

See, age is only heavy if you carry it like a weight. When you wear it like wisdom, it becomes your fuel. I might have a few more grays and a little more stretch in my mornings, but I also have clarity I never had at twenty, courage I didn't have at thirty, and peace I was still chasing at forty.

Back in the day, growing up in Chicago, I didn't see many examples of people thriving in their fifties. Most people I knew were already worn down by life—jobs that broke their bodies, relationships that broke their hearts, and dreams they buried in silence. I watched men give up without even realizing they had done so. They'd sit on the porch, beer in hand, eyes glazed over, talking about "back in the day" like their future no longer existed.

I told myself, *"I don't want that to be me."* Truthfully, I didn't always believe I could be different. I carried so many false timelines in my head. I thought if I didn't "make it" by thirty, I was behind. If I wasn't rich by forty, I would have failed. If I hadn't figured it all out by forty-five, maybe I never would.

That's the lie society feeds us—especially as Black men: We are destined to expire early. Our pain is permanent. Our creativity has an expiration date. Let me tell you something: God doesn't run on your timeline or society's clock. He's eternal. If you're still breathing, He still has something for you.

I'm an entrepreneur now, but that journey didn't start with a business plan. It started with me not fitting into boxes. I was that kid who didn't sit still, talked too much, and asked "why" one too many times in class. I always had ideas and a hustle, but I didn't have direction. Truthfully, I didn't have mentorship either. Nobody told me I was a visionary. They said I was "doing too much."

Yet even back then, I was dreaming.

I remember making meals for my family as a kid—not because I wanted to be a chef, but because it gave me peace. There was something sacred about feeding people—about turning nothing into something. Now I see how God was planting seeds of BreakinBread21 before I even knew what entrepreneurship was. I didn't go to business school. Life was my classroom. Pain was my professor. Grace was my tutor.

There were times I wanted to quit. Businesses failed. Events flopped. Clients ghosted me. People talked behind my back. Yeah, I made some wrong turns, but each time, God used it. Every breakdown built my backbone.

And today? I'm not just a chef. I'm a storyteller. I'm a healer through food. I'm a creator of experiences. I'm proof that even when the world says you're "too late," God says, "I'm right on time."

Let me say this clearly: It's never too late to reintroduce yourself to the world—and to yourself.

You can be thirty or sixty and still launch that dream.
You can be divorced and still find love.
You can be broke and still build wealth.
You can be stuck and still start again.
You can be scared and still say yes.

The enemy loves to use age as an excuse. "You missed your window," he whispers, but let me tell you—when you walk with God, your window is never closed. You're not behind. You're in process, and everything you've gone through is part of the recipe.

God doesn't need your perfect past—He only needs your present "yes." As long as you're breathing, your purpose is still active. It's never too late to start, to grow, to become. The moment you decide to detox from delay and doubt, divine acceleration begins.

You are not expired—you are evolving. I've watched too many people let time punk them out of their promise. They stopped learning. Stopped dreaming. Started saying, "*It is what it is*" instead of "*It could be what I make it.*" However, I'm here to wake you up and remind you of who you are.

You were born with purpose, and purpose doesn't age out. So rise up. Reignite your vision. Go back to school. Start the business. Write the book. Say yes to the calling. Become the version of yourself that your younger self needed to see.

Do it now. Not just for you but for your kids and your kids' kids. Because when you start believing again, you're teaching your family what's possible at any age. Let your children see you dream out loud. Let them see you take risks, laugh hard, heal deeply, and walk boldly. Let them witness what freedom looks like in a grown man's body. That's legacy.

I'm fifty, and I feel like I'm just starting to scratch the surface of my assignment: I'm still learning, still healing, still becoming. And you can, too, because the truth is this: if you've still got breath in your lungs, you still have a future in front of you.

So take a deep breath and begin again.

Chapter 7 Reflection

It's Never Too Late–Reclaiming Time, Purpose, and Possibility

Regret is heavy—but hope is healing. Chapter 7 reminded you that no matter how much time you feel you've lost, the moment you decide to change, **everything changes**. It's never too late to detox. Never too late to restart. Never too late to rise again. This chapter calls you to embrace grace over guilt and progress over perfection.

You are not behind. You're right on time—because you're moving now.

Reflection Questions

1. What dreams or goals have I given up on because I thought it was "too late"?

2. What lies have I believed about missed opportunities or wasted time?

3. What lesson has taken me the longest to learn—but I finally understand now?

4. How can I make the most of the time I have left with purpose and clarity?

5. What "unfinished business" do I now feel empowered to address or complete?

6. Who or what has been waiting on me to rise up, heal, or lead?

7. In what ways can my comeback be a testimony to someone else's breakthrough?

8. What new belief will I carry moving forward about timing, purpose, and grace?

It's Never Too Late
Daily Practices to Redeem the Time

Every day is a new invitation to rebuild, restore, and realign. These practices will help you walk boldly into the "now," without being held hostage by the "before."

1. Morning Reset Declaration

Start your day with this truth:

> *"I am not late. I am aligned. Today is the perfect time to move forward."*

Say it out loud. Say it with faith. Let it shift your mindset.

2. One Act of Forward Motion

Each day, choose one small action that honors your next chapter:

- Make the call.

- Apply for the opportunity.

- Start writing the book.

- Sign up for the class.

- Pray over the vision.

Progress, not perfection.

3. Reflect and Reframe

Take five minutes to journal:

> *"What did I learn from what I thought I lost?"*

Turn pain into purpose by acknowledging the growth that came with delay.

4. Celebrate Your Now

Each evening, write down one thing you did *today* that your old self would have avoided, ignored, or procrastinated on.

Let your daily wins become a new pattern of confidence.

5. Weekly Redemption Practice

At the end of each week, ask yourself:

> *"What would it look like if I gave myself full permission to begin again?"*

Write your answer. Then commit to acting on one piece of it in the upcoming week.

Closing Reminder

God doesn't need your perfect past—He only needs your present "yes." As long as you're breathing, your purpose is still active. It's never too late to start, to grow, to become. The moment you decide to detox from delay and doubt, **divine acceleration** begins.

CHAPTER 8

IT'S NEVER TOO EARLY TO TEACH THE LEGACY

"Train up a child in the way he should go, and when he is old, he will not depart from it."

—Proverbs 22:6

Let me say this loud and clear:

We are not just healing for ourselves—we are healing for them: for the little ones watching, the teenagers questioning, and the young adults searching for something real, something rooted, something bigger than followers and fame.

We live in a world that's moving fast: so much noise, so much influence, so much confusion disguised as confidence. Make no mistake. If we don't teach them early, the world will teach them anyway, and we *don't* want that.

This generation is unlike any I've ever seen. Man … they're bold. They're expressive. They're building apps in middle school, launching brands out of their bedrooms, and investing in crypto before they even open a savings account. They have access, connection, and reach, but so many are missing *direction*. They're powerful, but misaligned. Creative, but anxious. Gifted, but unsure of who gave them the gift.

Now imagine—just imagine—if we could meet them early with clarity, identity, healing, and purpose. What if they didn't have to unlearn what we had to unlearn? What if they didn't have to detox at thirty, forty, or fifty because they started the detox young? What if their first mentors were fully healed and honest?

That's What Legacy Looks Like

I'll be straight up with you: Growing up, I didn't have a legacy manual—I had survival. I had hustle. I had prayer, but I also had confusion. I didn't know how to process emotions, handle money, honor my health, or create a vision that extended beyond the moment. I had dreams but didn't always believe I had the tools to reach them.

I made many mistakes—not because I was a bad kid, but because *no one taught me early*. No one taught me how to detox the pain I inherited. No one explained what healing could look like. I saw broken men model broken behavior and call it "being a man." I watched people bury dreams and call it "real life." I was surrounded by silence when I needed structure.

So, I grew up figuring it out the hard way.

That's why this matters so much to me now. That's why I'm writing this book.
That's why I'm building these businesses.
That's why I pour into my children.
That's why I speak, serve, share, and show up even when I'm tired.

Because I know what it's like to be a child with no compass, and I refuse to let the next generation grow up without direction. It's never too early to plant the seeds of a legacy.

Legacy isn't about money. It's not just what we leave *for* them. It's what we leave **in** them. It's the values. The wisdom. The principles. The purpose. The foundation that will hold them steady when the world starts shaking.

You don't have to be rich to teach legacy. You don't have to be famous to pour into the next generation. You only have to be available.

Pull them aside. Tell them the truth. Don't sugarcoat it. Tell them what inevitably happens when you don't deal with trauma. Tell them what happens when you don't know your worth, don't tithe, chase validation, and confuse attention with affection. Tell them what happens when you wake up at fifty, feeling like your life just started because you didn't have guidance at fifteen.

Then, tell them this: *you don't have to wait to get it right.*

You can detox now.
You can choose differently now. You can build healthy habits now. You can set boundaries now.
You can love yourself fully—*now*.

That's what I want to give my children. That's what I want to give YOUR children. I'm launching this movement—this D.E.T.O.X. Journey—to become a *blueprint,* a *bridge,* a *baton.*

The goal is not just to be the one who broke the curse. The goal is to raise children who *don't have to recover from their parents.*

Let that sink in.

If we give them this gift early—this mindset, this faith, this emotional intelligence, this financial literacy, this health consciousness—they'll grow into leaders who don't lead from pain. They'll build from love, not lack. They'll walk with authority, not anxiety.

They'll be the healed generation we prayed for.

So let's teach them to detox spiritually—so they don't get spiritually lost.
Let's teach them to detox mentally—so they don't suffer silently.
Let's teach them to detox physically—so their health doesn't become a future prison.
Let's teach them to detox financially—so they can fund their purpose, not just flex.
Let's teach them to detox socially—so they choose alignment over attention.

We're not just raising kids anymore. We're raising kings.
We're raising queens.
We're raising visionaries, disruptors, creators, healers, and legacy builders.

However, it starts with us. We can't pass on what we haven't practiced. We can't teach what we haven't lived. So, let your life be the curriculum. You're the walking syllabus—let them study you.

I'm not perfect. I still mess up, but I'm honest about my mistakes. I let my kids see me heal in real time. I let them see me chase purpose after pain. I let them know what it looks like to rebuild and reinvent.

That transparency? That's leadership.

They don't need us to be superheroes. They only need us to be **REAL**: *present, consistent,* and willing to pass on what we've learned before they have to learn it the hard way.

So listen up to every parent, mentor, big brother, auntie, teacher, coach, and community leader:

Legacy starts with you. It lives through them—and the time to teach it is NOW. It's never too early to start planting, because the seeds you sow today? That's someone's future fruit.

CHAPTER 8 REFLECTION
It's Never Too Early to Teach the Legacy— Living What You Want to Leave

Legacy isn't what you leave behind—it's what you live out daily. Chapter 8 reminded you that every action, every word, and every sacrifice shapes the blueprint others will follow. Whether you're raising children, mentoring others, or simply showing up in your community, you are a living legacy.

You don't have to wait until you're old to pass something on. The time to teach, model, and deposit wisdom is now.

Reflection Questions

1. What values do I want to be remembered for—and am I living them now?

2. What habits, mindset, or language do I need to detox so I don't pass them down?

3. Who in my life is watching me—even if they never say it?

4. What's one story or lesson from my life that I need to start sharing more intentionally?

5. Have I taken time to ask my elders what legacy they want to leave?

6. What does it mean for me to "live" legacy rather than only "leave" legacy?

7. What seeds am I planting today that will outlive me?

8. What is the spiritual, emotional, or financial inheritance I want to pass on?

It's Never Too Early to Teach the Legacy
Daily Practices to Build a Life That Speaks

Legacy is created in the small moments—in what we teach, model, and repeat. These daily actions will help you cultivate a lifestyle that leaves a mark of faith, love, and wisdom.

1. Lead by Example (Even When No One's Watching)

Ask: *"If someone followed my actions today, what would they learn?"*

Be the standard before you speak it.

2. Teach Through Testimony

Share one story from your life each week with someone younger—about failure, faith, or resilience. Don't wait for the perfect moment.

> *Legacy is learned through real life, not rehearsed lectures.*

3. Intentional Deposits

Each day, pour into someone—even in small ways:

- A word of encouragement

- A scripture or quote

- A skill you've learned

- A call to check in

Be the mentor you wish you had.

4. Record the Wisdom

Start a "Legacy Journal" to record prayers, lessons, letters to loved ones, or powerful truths. This becomes a blueprint your family or community can carry forward.

5. Practice Generational Thinking

Before you make a major decision, ask:

"Will this bless the generation behind me—or burden them?"

Let legacy lead your choices.

Closing Reminder

Legacy doesn't start in a will—it starts in your will to live with intention. It's never too early to teach. It's never too early to build. And it's never too early to become the example you wish you had. You are not just building for today—you are planting for tomorrow.

CHAPTER 9

ME VERSUS ME

"Do not conform to the pattern of this world, but be transformed by the renewing of your mind. T hen you will be able to test and approve what God's will is—His good, pleasing and perfect will."

—Romans 12:2 (NIV)

It became mine.

Every move I made, especially early on in my entrepreneurial grind, was me trying to prove something. Not to the world. Not to the haters. But to that damn voice. I was out here trying to "get it right," wearing myself out, chasing perfection, and hiding my pain behind success. I'd look around and think, *Yo, why do I still feel empty when I should be celebrating?* It's because I wasn't building for me—I was building to silence something I never questioned.

That showed up everywhere. In business. In fatherhood. In my marriage. In my friendships. Even when I was doing "good," that inner critic would whisper, *But is it enough?* Man, I used to look at my kids—beautiful blessings—and still feel like I was failing them because I couldn't always give what I didn't even receive. That right there? That was the most painful part.

Only then came the shift—the detox.

One day, I had to stop and say, *"Hold up. This ain't even me talking. It is years of other people's pain sitting in my mind rent-free. It is trauma trying to set up shop in my identity."* I had to strip all that off.

D.E.T.O.X. ain't just about your body. It's about your thoughts. Your spirit. Your habits. And it starts with getting honest. Real honest. I had to sit with my own truth and ask, *"Who told you that you weren't enough? Who gave you that story? Why are you still reading from that old script?"*

I realized I was fighting a version of myself that never existed—a version shaped by fear, by disappointment, by unhealed wounds. I had to let that version die so I could truly live. Not just exist—live. Boldly. Authentically. Freely.

I started pouring time into myself—mind, body, and spirit. I began unlearning the lies and rewriting the narrative—one step at a time. I still hear that old voice some days, but now, I talk back. I remind myself, *"You are chosen. You are called. You are becoming."*

That light that folks used to talk about? That energy people say I carry when I walk into a room? I didn't see it for a long time. I used to think they were just being nice. Yet that light? That spirit? It's real. It's divine. It's the essence of who I am.

You know what? It was always there: buried beneath trauma, drowned out by noise, but never gone.

I'm still learning to trust it, to lead with it, to protect it. Now that I see it myself, I don't need anybody to confirm it. Not my family. Not society. Not culture. Not even my past. That's the power of detox—getting rid of everything keeping you from your own light.

Believe me, I ain't done. I'm still in it. One day at a time, I'm detoxing—mentally, spiritually, physically, financially, socially. Every day, I choose to grow with the world, not against it. I choose alignment over hustle. Peace over performance. Purpose over pressure.

See, here's what genuinely changed the game for me: realizing that most people who didn't see my light couldn't even see their own. Family, friends, mentors—some couldn't pour into me because they were empty, and I no longer blame them. Hurt people hurt people. Lost people can't guide others. I had to stop expecting people to give me what they had never received.

That, fam, is when I took my power back.

To the next generation reading this: I see you. I feel you. I need you to hear me when I say your light is real. Your battles are valid, but don't let those battles define you. You are not your trauma. You are not your mistakes. You are not what they said about you. You are becoming something greater.

You are choosing to break cycles. To heal the bloodline. To raise the vibration.

Bottom line? You gotta detox. You gotta shed the lies, the pain, the false identities. Because when you do? When you fight the "Me versus Me" battle with truth, love, and faith?

You don't just win—you transform.

So yeah, I'm still in the fight. I have days when the old me tries to return, knocking on the door. However, now I answer with wisdom. I answer with purpose. I answer with truth because I ain't who I used to be—and I ain't done evolving either.

This journey is personal, but it's universal, too. We're all in this together, just at different stages. So, if you're reading this and feel like you're battling yourself right now, please know—you ain't alone. Keep going. Keep healing. Keep becoming.

This is the D.E.T.O.X. Journey—Me Versus Me—and I'm winning, one day at a time.

CHAPTER 9 REFLECTION
Me Versus Me–Conquering the Inner Critic

Sometimes the loudest battle isn't outside—it's the war within. In Chapter 9, "Me Versus Me," you confronted the truth that the person who has the most power to build or break you … IS you. The inner critic, the self-doubt, the perfectionism, the fear—they don't always come from others. Often, they come from learned patterns that replay in your mind on repeat.

The most powerful detox is the one that frees you from *you*—so your healed self can lead your future.

Reflection Questions

1. What is the most common lie I tell myself—or have believed about myself for years?

2. What's one moment in my past that shaped how I see myself today?

3. How do I typically talk to myself when I make a mistake? Is it with grace or criticism?

4. What fear keeps showing up disguised as "logic" or "wisdom"?

5. Am I addicted to proving myself—or becoming myself?

6. What would my life look like if I stopped getting in my own way?

7. Who am I when I'm free from fear, insecurity, or comparison?

8. What does the healed version of me believe—and how does that version behave?

Me Versus Me
Daily Practices to Win the Inner Battle

You are not your mistakes. You are not your trauma. You are not your past voice. These daily actions are designed to help you detox from self-sabotage and emerge as your empowered, renewed self—one day at a time.

1. Morning Mirror Truth

Each morning, stand in front of a mirror and say:

> *"Today, I choose to believe in the version of me that God sees—not the version my fears created."*

Say it out loud until your inner voice adjusts to the new frequency.

2. Interrupt the Inner Critic

When a negative thought comes up, pause and ask:

"Is this thought based on truth—or trauma?"

Then reframe it with compassion:

- From *"I'm a failure"* → *"I'm still learning."*

- From *"No one sees me"* → *"God sees me, and my voice matters."*

3. Empowered Self-Journaling

Write a letter **from** your healed future self **to** your current self. Let it speak vision, confidence, and clarity into your now.

4. Move Through Resistance

Each day, do **one thing you've been avoiding** because of fear, procrastination, or doubt.

Small wins build new confidence.

5. Forgive Yourself—Out Loud

End your day with:

"I forgive myself for _____. I'm learning, growing, and healing forward."

Healing accelerates when you release self-punishment.

Closing Reminder

The real battle isn't about proving others wrong—it's about proving your healed self right. When you confront the version of you that's been surviving, doubting, and shrinking, you make space for the version that's destined, disciplined, and free. This is your comeback. However, this time, it's ***you versus the healed you—and the healed you wins***.

CHAPTER 10

PLAIN SIGHT— THE POWER OF POSITIVE WORDS

"The tongue has the power of life and death, and those who love it will eat its fruit."

— Proverbs 18:21 (NIV)

Let me tell you something real.

Everything we need—every answer, every opportunity, every breakthrough—has been right in front of us this whole time. The crazy thing is that most of us are too distracted, too wounded, or too caught up in survival mode to even *see* it. I used to think I had to chase blessings down, run to new cities, cut everybody off, and switch up everything around me to feel like I was getting somewhere.

Turns out life—*God*—taught me differently. Sometimes, what you need isn't a change of scenery. It's a change in how you look at things.

This chapter is personal, man, because it came from a moment where I had to stop everything and realize that I'd been walking past gold, trying to find silver. I was waiting for some grand sign, some big breakthrough, but the truth? The truth was already there, sitting in *plain sight,* but I wasn't looking through healed eyes. I was seeing life through a cracked lens—trauma, fear, pressure, doubt.

That's when it clicked.

If I wanted to detox my life—spiritually, mentally, physically, financially, socially—I had to start with my *words*. What I was saying, what I was hearing, what I was letting stick to my spirit. You can't grow out here eating poison, fam. You gotta feed your mind the truth—daily. I'm talkin' real, powerful affirmations that align you with who God says you are, not who the world tried to convince you to be.

So, I started writing positive words everywhere. Sticky notes, index cards, whiteboards in my kitchen, and even my phone lock screen. Stuff like:

- *You're Chosen*

- *Keep Going*

- *God's Plan > Your Fears*

- *Peace Over Pressure*

Every day, I made sure the first thing I saw when I woke up and the last thing I saw before I lay my head down was the truth. Not IG. Not bad news. Not bills. *Truth.* Because that's how you rewire your brain. That's how you break curses. That's how you shift perspective.

Let me break this down even deeper.

Words Heal, Words Hurt, and Words Also Build

Coming up, I didn't always hear the most uplifting stuff. A lot of us didn't. My old man, God rest his soul, was a tough one. Old school. Discipline over dialogue. I heard more criticism than encouragement. That mess sticks with you. As a young Black man, you internalize that. Then you grow up still trying to earn a "good job" or an "I'm proud of you" from a voice that's no longer even speaking.

It wasn't just him. I had teachers, coaches, and even "friends" who said things that made me question if I was enough. That voice—the one that says, *You're not ready, You're not built for this,* or *You'll mess this up like last time*—wasn't mine.

So I replaced it. I started speaking *life* over myself.
I'm talking, standing in the mirror like—
"Nah, Chef Harry, you're **that guy.**
You were chosen for this.
You walk in purpose.
You bring healing when you cook.
You inspire people just by being you."

I ain't gonna lie—it felt weird at first. As if I were faking, but eventually, those words took root. And once they did, *everything* around me started shifting.

Business started moving. My creativity leveled up. I started attracting better clients, better energy, and even better conversations. I started leading with peace instead of panic.

The D.E.T.O.X. is Daily

I need y'all to hear this loud: This D.E.T.O.X. Journey ain't a one-and-done type of thing. It is a *daily walk.* One day at a time, I'm shedding layers—old habits, false beliefs, toxic relationships, negative talk. I'm not perfect, but I'm *intentional,* and that's what counts.

The detox is in the *doing*, not just the dreaming.

Right now, I'm still walking it out.

- **Spiritually**—I'm spending more quiet time with God.
- **Mentally**—I'm protecting my peace like it's money in the safe.
- **Physically**—I'm eating clean, moving daily, and honoring this temple.
- **Financially**—I'm stewarding what I have with wisdom.
- **Socially**—I'm checking my circle, making sure iron's sharpening iron.

You gotta speak what you seek until you see what you said. That's the detox. That's the power of positive words.

Here's Some Gems I Keep in Front of Me Every Day:

1. **You have four types of people in your life: they either add to you, subtract from you, multiply your joy, or divide your peace.** This is a powerful reminder that everyone who enters your life serves a purpose, whether positive or negative. You get to choose what you allow in your space, which affects everything related to your growth. The key is knowing when to release the things that subtract from you and multiply the things that add value.

2. **You cannot put a question mark behind God's period.** This one hit me hard. I spent too many years questioning my path, doubting the purpose in my life. When I stopped second-guessing God's plan for me, things began to shift. Trusting His plan is a game-changer.

3. **He who throws dirt loses ground.**
   So many of us waste time worrying about what others think or say. The truth is that those who attempt to bring you down are only digging a pit for themselves. You keep moving forward and watch how quickly they get stuck in the mess they tried to create for you.

4. **Don't mistake habit for hard work.**
   It's easy to fall into the trap of doing things simply because they've become routine. Be aware that these routine tasks do not mean you're growing or moving forward. Actual progress comes from intentional action—not just mindless effort.

5. **Your gift will make room for you and put you in the presence of great men.**
   There is power in recognizing your unique gift, no matter how small it may seem. It will open doors you never imagined possible and connect you with people who can elevate your life.

6. **Sometimes, you don't jump—you get pushed to your purpose because of your fear of not succeeding.**
   Let's be honest: fear holds us back. Yet sometimes, when we don't take the leap, life pushes us right into the core purpose we're scared to pursue. Don't wait for that push. Start moving forward, even if it's small steps.

7. **Dirty water doesn't stop plants from growing, so don't let negative words stop you from your growth.**
   Negative people will always try to throw shade on your dreams. Much like plants grow through dirt and rain, you, too, can grow through negativity. Your potential is unstoppable—don't let anyone dim your light.

8. **Jealousy: Love and Hate, All at Once**
   If you've ever struggled with envy or resentment, this is a wake-up call. Jealousy is a mask for unhealed wounds. It's important to acknowledge this in yourself and release the grip of comparisons. There is space for all of us to succeed.

9. **The past is the past, and you will never get it back. Live for today.**
   Holding onto past mistakes or regrets only keeps you stuck. It's a constant weight that prevents you from moving forward. The best way to honor your past is to let it go and live fully in the present, where your power lies.

10. **It's the fourth quarter. The game is not over, no matter what the score is. Don't quit.**
    When you feel like giving up, remember this: The game isn't over until it's over. There's always time for a comeback. Remember that your breakthrough could be just around the corner, even when it feels like all hope is lost.

11. **They are watching. Stay focused.**
    There's always someone watching you—whether it's your children, peers, or even strangers. The example you set can impact more people than you know. Stay true to who you are, and let your focus drive you.

12. **Don't blend in—be somebody. Stand out.**
    It's easy to follow the crowd, to stay in the background. Despite your doubts, God has created you to be unique. Embrace your individuality because the world needs what only you can bring.

13. **Faith is a prerequisite for your purpose, and your purpose is power.**
    You cannot walk in your purpose without faith. The two go hand in hand. When you walk in faith, you unlock the power that has always been inside you. It's your secret weapon.

14. **Worrying is like paying a debt you don't owe. Let it go.**
    Everyone needs to hear this: stop worrying! It serves no purpose other than to drain your energy and focus. If it's not in your control—release it. Trust that God has it.

15. **Learn to love the sound of your feet walking away from things that no longer nourish your soul—it's Divine order.**
    Letting go of people, places, and things that no longer serve you can be a painful process. Yet there's peace in knowing you're moving toward what is destined for you. Embrace it.

16. **Fear is the assassin of faith.**
    Fear kills progress. Fear kills dreams. Fear kills purpose, whereas faith brings life. The more you choose faith over fear, the more you align with the life God has for you.

17. **God doesn't call the qualified—He qualifies the called.**
    So many of us wait until we feel "ready" or "good enough" before we walk into our purpose. Though if we're being honest, we'd never move if we waited until we felt worthy, reminding us that if God has placed something in your heart, He's not looking for perfection—He's looking for obedience. Your growth comes *through* the journey, not before it.

18. **Obedience is better than sacrifice.**
    We often confuse grinding, hustling, or overextending ourselves with being on the right path. Yet sometimes, the most powerful thing you can do is simply say *YES* to what God asked you to do the first time. You don't have to overcomplicate your calling. Obedience will open doors that sacrifice could never access.

19. **You can't heal what you hide.**
   This one sat with me heavily during my emotional and spiritual detox. I had buried things so deeply, thinking that if I didn't speak about them, they didn't exist. However, healing only begins when you're *honest* about what hurts. That's where freedom begins—in the light, not the shadows. Keep this truth in plain sight when the enemy tries to convince you to suffer in silence.

20. **If you don't transform your pain, you will transfer it.**
   This one hit me especially hard as a father, husband, and leader. I realized that unhealed trauma doesn't just disappear—it spills. It shows up in how we speak, how we love, how we lead, and even how we dream. Keeping this quote visible was a daily reminder that my healing wasn't just for me—it was for the people I love most.

Listen, fam, if you're trying to evolve, elevate, and live life fully—you *gotta* be mindful of the words you surround yourself with. Because what you keep in front of you … you eventually become. Speak life, speak purpose, and speak abundance. If you don't believe it yet, say it anyway. Say it until it's real.

This is how we rise. This is how we detox—one word at a time.

CHAPTER 10 REFLECTION
Plain Sight–The Power of Positive Words

Words shape worlds. Chapter 10 reminded you that life and death are in the power of the tongue. What you say about yourself, your circumstances, your future, and others has the power to either build or break, create or destroy. The words we speak (and think) form the reality we live in.

Positive words aren't just affirmations—they're spiritual agreements with purpose, healing, and identity.

Reflection Questions

1. What have I been speaking over myself lately—and is it building or breaking me?

2. What word or phrase from my past do I need to break from my vocabulary?

3. How do I speak to myself in private versus how I present myself in public?

4. Who's been shaped by my words—positively or negatively—and how can I restore or reinforce those impacts?

5. When was the last time I intentionally spoke life into my goals, relationships, or calling?

6. What lies have I repeated so often that they started to sound like truth?

7. If God recorded my words for one day, would they sound like faith—or fear?

8. What words do I need to start declaring daily over my life, family, and future?

Plain Sight
Daily Practices to Speak Life and Walk in Agreement

Your words are not just sounds—they are seeds. These daily practices will help you train your mind and mouth to align with purpose, peace, and power.

1. Daily Word Watch

Each day, be intentional about monitoring your words. When a negative or limiting statement slips out, pause and ask:

"Do I really want to plant that in my future?"

If not, replace it with a life-giving truth.

2. Speak Life Aloud

Every morning, declare out loud:

- *"I speak peace into my atmosphere."*

- *"I am aligned with the will of God for my life."*

- *"My words create doors, not walls."*

Speak it like you believe it—even before you feel it.

3. One Word of Encouragement

Each day, text, call, or compliment someone intentionally. Let your words become healing for others, too.

A positive word can be the seed of someone else's breakthrough.

4. Break the Agreement

Write down three negative words or phrases you've been speaking for years (about money, health, relationships, or purpose). Then pray or declare:

"I break the agreement with _____. I no longer accept that as truth in my life."

Rip up the paper as a symbolic act of release.

5. Evening Gratitude Recap

Each night, speak out loud three things you're grateful for. This rewires your language to focus on abundance instead of lack.

Closing Reminder

Your words are not invisible—they're creating your next visible season. Whether whispered in prayer or spoken in passing, what you say becomes what you see. Guard your mouth. Heal your language. Speak your life forward—on purpose.

CHAPTER 10
JOURNAL PAGE—PLAIN SIGHT

Create Your Vision-Rich Environment

Date: _____

Reflection Questions

1. What message have I been unintentionally keeping in front of me every day?
(This can be the energy of your environment, words people speak over you, or thoughts you've repeated.)

_____

_____

_____

2. How has that message shaped the way I see myself and my potential?

_____

_____

_____

3. What do I want to see, feel, or hear more of in my daily space and spirit? *(This is the emotional environment you want to walk in: peace, faith, love, purpose, clarity, etc.)*

_____

_____

_____

My Affirmations / Power Statements

Pull from quotes, scriptures, personal mantras—or use your own words. These should inspire, challenge, or affirm you.

1. _____
2. _____
3. _____
4. _____
5. _____
6. _____

Plain Sight Placement Plan

Where will you post or place your affirmations so you can see them every day? List at least three locations.

Example: Bathroom mirror
Example: Phone lock screen
Example: Rearview mirror in your car

- _____
- _____
- _____

Final Thought of the Day

Complete this sentence:

Today, I choose to believe that I am ...

_____
_____
_____

CHAPTER 11

THE LOST LEADING THE LOST

"Let them alone: they be blind leaders of the blind. And if the blind lead the blind, both shall fall into the ditch."

—Matthew 15:14 (KJV)

We are living in a time when influence is more accessible than ever before. However, purpose is more elusive. Every day, we see people with massive followings, loud voices, and bold opinions. Still, the question remains: Where are they leading us? Who are they following themselves?

Too many are leading others while they themselves are lost. No compass, no purpose, no foundation. It's like the blind leading the blind, and the result is a generation misled—not because they're incapable, but because the leaders themselves are still searching.

This chapter is not just a critique of today's culture—it's a call to accountability, a mirror moment. Before we take on the role of leader, teacher, influencer, parent, or guide, we must first ask ourselves: *Am I truly found? Do I know where I'm going? Do I know why I'm going there?*

The Truth About Misguided Leadership

Some of the people who seem the most confident, loud, or put together on the outside are often the most broken on the inside. They've mastered the art of the highlight reel, but they've neglected their own healing. They're teaching principles they haven't lived, preaching values they don't practice, and guiding people through paths they've never actually walked.

I was once one of them. I had the words. I had charisma. I had a presence. But I didn't have any healing. I didn't have the alignment. I didn't have the internal clarity. I was leading people, offering them advice, and motivating them while still battling demons I hadn't detoxed from.

We often inherit leadership roles without preparation. We become fathers, bosses, mentors, and influencers before we've truly processed our own trauma or found our direction. That's why detoxing is essential—not just for personal growth, but for responsible leadership as well.

The Ripple Effect

When a lost person leads another, it creates generational misguidance. One person's unhealed wounds can shape the mindsets of dozens—maybe hundreds. Think about the power of a teacher who doesn't believe in their students. A parent who's projecting pain onto their children. A spiritual leader who hasn't dealt with their own doubts.

When we don't take time to find ourselves, we pass down confusion. Yet when we do the work—when we detox spiritually, mentally, physically, financially, and socially—we become a beacon of light. We become the light others saw in us long before we saw it in ourselves. I always wondered what some elders were talking about when they looked at me and said, " You are special." I just had to dig in deep to find that "Special."

The Lost Leading the Lost

When I reflect on "the lost leading the lost," I think about how so many people are out here just talking—leading their children, their communities, their followers—without ever burying their own misconceptions about life. They haven't sat down to find their own truth—to ask what's real and what's been handed down to them.

So many people walk this earth never really being themselves, simply because they've never taken the time to find their purpose. They're just reenacting the cycles they were born into, playing out generational patterns that no longer serve their spirit.

It's just like the saying: *the blind leading the blind.* Except this time, it's *the lost leading the lost.*

That's why I had to confront the traditions I inherited from my West Indian upbringing. There were powerful morals and bold rules, yes—but there was also harshness in the tone, in the discipline, in the words. Words that, once translated from Creole to English, held meanings that tore down more than they built up. They damaged the fiber of who we were as kids.

Just because you're part of a family doesn't mean you must conform to traditions that don't align with your spirit. Once you find your purpose, your spirit will guide you when you feel the disconnect. That's when detox begins.

We have to be mindful of how we lead. We must first lead ourselves before we lead our children. We say the right things to them, we guide them, but if we haven't detoxed our own systems, we're passing down confusion instead of clarity. D.E.T.O.X. is how we ensure our children won't walk around lost in a world that already wants to pull them in a thousand directions. It's how we prepare them to walk boldly in who they are.

The Turning Point

Leadership starts with honesty. The moment I admitted I was lost was the moment I began to find my way. I had to strip away my ego and say, *"God, I don't want to mislead anyone else while I'm still trying to figure out who I am."* That surrender opened the door for true transformation.

This chapter reminds you that it's okay to be in the process, but while you're in that process, lead with transparency. Don't pretend to be whole—invite others into the healing journey with you. That's the kind of leadership this world needs.

We don't need perfect leaders. We need honest ones. Healed ones. Those who aren't afraid to say, "I was lost, but I'm finding my way—and you can too."

Reflection Questions:

1. Have you ever led someone while you felt lost yourself?
2. What impact did that have on your life and theirs?
3. What steps can you take today to become a more honest and healed leader?
4. Are there any roles you've taken on prematurely? How can you seek support in those areas?
5. What traditions or inherited beliefs no longer align with your spirit?
6. In what ways can you detox from them to become a more authentic leader?

Let this be the chapter that frees you from the pressure of perfection and invites you into the power of purpose. Find yourself first—then help others do the same.

Because found people … find people.

CHAPTER 11 REFLECTION
The Lost Leading the Lost–Healing Before You Guide

In this chapter, you confronted a difficult truth: many of us are trying to lead, mentor, or guide others while we ourselves are still bleeding. *The Lost Leading the Lost* is a sobering reminder that influence without healing is dangerous—not only for you, but for those watching and following you.

This chapter calls for reflection, humility, and the courage to pause and detox *before* stepping into leadership because healed leaders lead with clarity, not confusion.

Reflection Questions

1. Where in my life have I tried to lead others before fully confronting my own healing?

2. What kind of example am I currently setting—intentional or accidental?

3. How have I been projecting strength while privately struggling with my own direction?

4. Have I been seeking platforms more than wholeness? Why?

5. In what ways has unhealed leadership hurt me—or others under me?

6. What do I need to stop, surrender, or detox before I can lead with true integrity?

7. Am I leading people to God, healing, and truth—or to my own dysfunction and trauma response?

8. Who or what has been following my *unspoken* example—and how can I redirect them in truth?

The Lost Leading the Lost
Daily Practices to Heal Before You Guide

You don't need to be perfect to lead—but you do need to be **honest, accountable,** and **committed** to healing. These daily practices are designed to help you detox from performance-driven leadership and walk in purpose-driven influence.

1. Morning Mirror Truth

Say this aloud each morning:

> *"I cannot pour from an empty place. I will lead from overflow, not from a wound."*

Leadership starts with personal responsibility.

2. Self-Check Before You Speak

Before giving advice or direction to someone else, pause and ask:

> *"Have I lived or healed through this yet?"*

If not, lead them to God's Word or wise counsel—instead of leading from your pain.

3. Daily Leadership Audit

At the end of each day, journal:

> *"Did my words and actions today lead others toward healing—or confuse them?"*

Be honest. Adjust. Apologize if needed.

4. Pause and D.E.T.O.X.

Pick one day a week to pull back from public influence (social media, group chats, ministry, etc.) and pour into your soul.

Pray. Rest. Journal. Recalibrate.

> *A silent week can save a loud life from collapse.*

5. Find a Healing Mentor

Identify one person (a therapist, spiritual advisor, or trusted elder) who is pouring into you **consistently**.

> *You can't cover others well if no one is covering you.*

Closing Reminder

You don't need to have it all together to be a leader—but you **do** need to be committed to the process. Detoxing as a leader means stepping away from pride and into accountability. Because healed leaders don't just speak truth—they *embody* it. When you lead from a place of healing, you don't create followers—you create *freedom*.

CHAPTER 12

A WORLD OF PURPOSEFUL PEOPLE

"We have different gifts, according to the grace given to each of us. If your gift is prophesying, then prophesy in accordance with your faith; if it is serving, then serve; if it is teaching, then teach … if it is to lead, do it diligently; if it is to show mercy, do it cheerfully."

—Romans 12:6–8 (NIV)

Let me talk to you from the heart—straight up, no filters, no fancy wrapping. Just me, raw and authentic, walking in purpose, one step at a time. Because this thing called *life*, it ain't no highlight reel—it's a journey of constant detox, discovery, and divine design. When I picture a world full of people walking boldly in their purpose, using their God-given gifts with intention, I don't just see some utopia. I see *heaven touching Earth*. I see what we were created to be before trauma, comparison, fear, and culture told us otherwise. Growing up, I didn't have a perfect blueprint. I was raised in a Haitian household, where discipline was given with love, and purpose felt a lot like survival. I watched my family hustle, pray, and push through, but I didn't always see joy in the journey. I didn't know back then that purpose and peace could walk together.

Fast forward—I'm now a fifty-year-old man who's been broken and rebuilt more than once. A husband. A father. A chef. An entrepreneur. A man of God. Though more importantly, I'm *becoming*. Still evolving. Still healing. Still learning what it means to walk in purpose and teach others how to detox theirs into alignment.

And every single day, I choose to show up as a vessel—flawed but fueled by faith.

The Vision: A World Aligned in Purpose

Now imagine a world where everyone knows their lane and rides in it proudly. A world where nobody's out here chasing someone else's dream or trying to squeeze into someone else's calling. People would be too busy honoring their own gifts to get caught up in comparison.

Violence? Down. Jealousy? Irrelevant. Brokenness? Healed from the inside out. In this world, we'd see people with clarity—spiritually grounded, mentally focused, physically energized, financially abundant, and socially whole. Families would operate like legacy machines. Neighborhoods would be built on love, not lack. Kids would grow up seeing their parents *love their lives,* not just tolerate them.

This ain't no fantasy. It's the real promise when people choose to detox their lives and walk in purpose.

Divine Connections, Not Coincidences

I've experienced divine alignment in ways that still give me chills. I've met people who felt like missing pieces of my puzzle. They didn't come to take—they came to build. Because when you're walking in purpose, your energy shifts. You attract people on the same frequency. You speak a language that only purpose-driven folks can hear.

Let me tell you something: when you recognize your gift and choose to activate it, you become a *magnet* for alignment. Every chef has a taste. Every artist has a stroke. Every speaker has a tone. Every leader has a pace. Whatever your gift is, the world is waiting for you to stop sleeping on it and *show up*.

The D.E.T.O.X. Blueprint That Changed My Life

Now, I can't speak on purpose without speaking about *detox*. That's been my blueprint. It's not just some catchy acronym—it's how I saved myself.

- **Spiritually**, I had to reconnect with God and stop performing religion. I needed a relationship.
- **Mentally**, I had to quiet the noise: old beliefs, old wounds, old stories that no longer served me.
- **Physically**, I had to honor my body—not just as a chef, but as a vessel. Health became my wealth.
- **Financially**, I had to shift from hustle to harmony. Money stopped owning me once I saw it as a tool, not a god.
- **Socially**, I had to clean house. The wrong circles will have you second-guessing your destiny.

Each area required my surrender. Trust me—it's still a process. I'm not on the mountaintop yelling down. I'm in the valley with you, climbing one step at a time.

Gifts Are for Giving

People love to say, "Everybody's got a gift." Yet how many of us honestly believe that about ourselves if we're being real? How many of us dig deep enough to *find* that gift, develop it, protect it, and put it to work?

It took me years to fully embrace mine. Cooking was always in me. Feeding people and creating experiences—that was my love language. Even so, it wasn't until I aligned it with purpose that it started feeding *me*. The business, the brand, and the doors that opened all came after the clarity. Once I got spiritually fed, the overflow hit every other area of my life.

You start walking differently. You no longer thirst for applause—you focus on assignment. You're not chasing trends—you're building a legacy. Every day you wake up, you ask, "Who can I serve with what I've been given?"

That's what purpose feels like.

Who I Am and Where I'm Headed

So here I stand. Not perfect. Not finished. But faithful. I know who I am. I know who I belong to. I know I was created for *more,* not just for me but for the people connected to my assignment.

I'm still detoxing. Still learning. Still letting go of things that can't come with me into this next season. Except now I've tasted purpose, I can't go back to living on autopilot. This ain't about titles or trophies. It's about transformation.

This is not the end of my story. It's just another chapter. Another chance to say *yes* to God. Another reminder that the world doesn't need more noise—it needs more *light.*

You Are the Beginning

A world of purposeful people doesn't start with a movement. It begins with a moment. One decision. One detox. One person—*you*—is choosing to live intentionally.

I chose purpose. I chose healing. I chose to lead from a place of authenticity. My prayer is that as you close this chapter, you choose the same. This is your invitation to wake up your gift. To believe that you were born for *such a time as this,* commit to the work, and trust the process.

The world is starving for people who aren't just successful but *significant.*

Welcome to a world of purposeful people. It begins with you.

CHAPTER 12 REFLECTION
A World of Purposeful People–Living the Lifestyle of D.E.T.O.X.

This final chapter is not just a conclusion—it's a commission.

A World of Purposeful People invites you to imagine what the world would look like if more people detoxed—spiritually, mentally, physically, financially, and socially—and truly lived in purpose. The goal of this journey was never just self-improvement. It was a *world transformation*, one healed life at a time.

When we detox our lives, we don't just become better individuals—we become better leaders, parents, partners, creators, and disciples. The lifestyle of D.E.T.O.X. is about *sustained alignment* with purpose and peace.

Reflection Questions

1. How has this D.E.T.O.X. Journey changed the way I see myself, others, and the world?

2. What does it mean to me to live a life of purpose—not just achievement?

3. Which D.E.T.O.X. pillar (spiritual, mental, physical, financial, or social) do I now feel called to help others grow in?

4. What habits and rhythms must I commit to in order to protect this lifestyle of clarity, peace, and power?

5. How can I serve others with what I've learned—without burning out or being performative?

6. Who in my life needs to start their own detox, and how can I lead them by example?

7. Am I willing to live this publicly and privately, even when it's inconvenient or uncomfortable?

8. What legacy do I want to leave in this world, and am I living that legacy *now*?

A World of Purposeful People
Daily Practices to Walk in the D.E.T.O.X. Lifestyle

This is no longer a challenge—it's a calling. These daily practices will help you maintain the lifestyle of detoxed living, purpose-driven focus, and kingdom-aligned influence.

1. Begin With Purpose

Each morning, ask:

> *"Who do I need to be today to stay aligned with purpose?"*

Let that question shape your tone, your tasks, and your time.

2. Share Your Oil

Every day, be intentional about pouring into one person:

- A word of encouragement

- A spiritual check-in

- A lesson you've learned from detox

- A bold truth said in love

Purposeful people don't hoard wisdom—they distribute it.

3. D.E.T.O.X. Check-In

Ask yourself at day's end:

- **Spiritually**—*"Did I hear from God today?"*

- **Mentally**—*"Did I protect my peace?"*

- **Physically**—*"Did I honor my body with rest or movement?"*

- **Financially**—*"Did I manage or waste resources?"*

- **Socially**—*"Did I connect with truth or tolerate toxicity?"*

4. Weekly Alignment Time

Each week, block time to journal, reflect, and reset. Review goals, track habits, and pray for continued alignment. Let this detox become a discipline.

5. Create Community

You don't have to walk this lifestyle alone. Build or join a group of like-minded, purpose-driven individuals who are also committed to detoxing and growing.

> *A healed world begins with healed people who walk in purpose—together.*

Closing Reminder

You are now part of something bigger than a book. You are part of a movement. A movement of people choosing clarity over confusion, purpose over performance, and healing over hiding. You are walking proof that when one life changes, it touches hundreds more.

So go—
Live the lifestyle.
Be the light.
Be the difference.
Be the detox.

CONCLUSION

This journey, this detox, is not just my story. It's a shared story—of transformation, growth, and rebirth. As I've walked through the stages of spiritual, mental, physical, financial, and social detox, it became more than just a personal challenge. It became a calling, a purpose, and a mission. I've been made new. More importantly, I've been made aware. Aware of how deeply these areas of our lives influence everything we touch. Aware of the power we hold when we choose to align ourselves with God's vision.

To the readers—this is your journey, too. No matter where you are in life, how old or young you are, or how much you've been through, ***it is never too late***. It's never too late to reset. It's never too late to heal. It's never too late to start over. God's time is perfect, and all things are possible in Him.

I pray this book serves as a guiding light for anyone who needs it. As you go through your own detox process, I want you to remember that *you are not alone*. The road may be challenging, but the reward is so much greater. I encourage you to keep going, to keep believing, and to keep reaching higher.

I dedicate this book to my God, who dropped this on me and continues to guide my path.

To my family:
I give thanks for their love, support, and patience as I've grown.

To Pastor Smokie Norful:
Thank you for your spiritual guidance and leadership throughout my D.E.T.O.X. Journey. Your shepherding through the Word and your daily example have been a beacon of light, helping me grow deeper in faith and clarity. Your influence has been invaluable in shaping my spiritual walk.

To Raina Kilgore, my therapist:
Thank you for helping me open my mind and heal my heart in ways I never imagined. Your guidance created space for breakthrough, restoration, and profound transformation. Your impact on my healing journey is lasting and invaluable.

To Mr. Kevin Davis and Reggie Byrd (Bird's Nest): Thank you for your unwavering support, belief, and brotherhood. Your presence reminded me of my light when I couldn't see it for myself. You not only encouraged my spirit but helped me discover my physical threshold and push beyond it. This journey would not be complete without honoring your impact.

To Mr. William Roundtree and the REI90 team:
Thank you for equipping me with financial strategies that became a turning point in my journey. Your teachings have laid a strong foundation for my road to financial success, and your impact continues to shape my mindset, habits, and future.

To my healthy circle of friends and influencers:
Thank you for standing by me, even when our relationships faced challenges. Your presence, prayers, and persistence taught me how to be

stronger, how to lean deeper into God, and how to shift my perspective when it mattered most. Iron truly sharpens iron, and I'm better because of you.

To Laray and Debbie Williams:
My bonus father and mother—thank you for choosing me, accepting me, and pouring scripture and unconditional love into my life. Your presence reminded me that family is not just by blood, but by God's divine assignment.

To my mother: Gizelle Jean-Simon
Thank you for your relentless work ethic, your passion for doing what you love, and for passing me the fork—both literally and figuratively. Your strength, perseverance, and unwavering spirit continue to inspire me daily. You will always be a part of who I am, in and out of the kitchen.

To my children, Jasmine, Kayla, RJ, and Myla:
Thank you for showing me what resilience and consistency truly look like through your growth and accomplishments. Each of you carries a unique gift the world deeply needs. You are my inspiration, my motivation, and most of all, my legacy. Keep shining. The world is better because you're in it.

To my wife: Vanassa
Thank you for being my partner, my accountability coach, and my greatest supporter. Your no-nonsense love and unwavering belief have been the steady hand guiding me through life's challenges. Though the journey has had its tough moments, together we always find our way back to joy in God's grace. You saw a potential in me that sometimes felt like it took a lifetime to uncover. You deserve the very best of me.

I pray that this book serves as a foundation for your life's detox. May it inspire you to lead your life with purpose, passion, and power.

Personal Prayer

Dear God,

I come before you humbly, grateful for the transformation you've allowed in my life. Thank you

for guiding me through the detox of my spirit, mind, body, finances, and social environment. Thank you for the lessons, the struggles, and the victories. You've shown me that in everything, there is growth. And through your grace, I've learned to see the beauty in the struggle.

I pray for every reader who opens these pages. May they find the courage to embark on their own D.E.T.O.X. Journey. May their hearts be open to change and feel Your presence every step of the way. I ask for strength for those who are struggling, vision for those who feel lost, and peace for those who are weary.

Lord, may this book serve as a beacon of hope to anyone who believes it's too late to change or too hard to start over. You've proven time and time again that with You, all things are possible.

Thank you for being the true detox in our lives. We trust in Your timing, Your purpose, and Your love.

In Jesus' name,

Amen

BIOGRAPHY

Harry Jean-Simon is a private chef, entrepreneur, speaker, and visionary hailing from Chicago, Illinois, with Haitian roots. As the founder of BreakinBread21 LLC and partner of Breath Of Fresh Air Travel, Harry infuses his cultural heritage and life experiences into every plate he serves and every story he tells. With over two decades of experience in the culinary industry and a passion for personal transformation, Harry has dedicated his life to helping others detox and enhance their spiritual, mental, physical, financial, and social well-being. He is also the host of the *D.E.T.O.X. with Chef Harry* podcast and the creator of the Elite Performance D.E.T.O.X. Challenge programs, where he mentors others through their healing journeys. Harry lives by faith, leads with purpose, and believes that with proper alignment, anything is possible.

Book Information

Title: *D.E.T.O.X.: 5 Ways to Cleanse Your Life and Find Your Purpose*

Author Name: Harry Jean-Simon

Co-Author Name (if applicable): N/A

Book Description:

D.E.T.O.X.: Five Ways to Cleanse Your Life and Find Your Purpose is a deeply personal and transformational guide inspired by Harry Jean-Simon's journey from pain to purpose. Drawing from his upbringing, entrepreneurial path, and spiritual journey, this book explores how to detox your life across five essential areas: **Spiritual**, **Mental**, **Physical**, **Financial**, and **Social**.

Using a blend of storytelling, biblical wisdom, journal-style reflection, and practical steps, Harry walks readers through the seasons of his life—from childhood challenges to adult awakenings and from moments of clarity to continuous growth. Each chapter aligns with one of the five areas of detox and shows how these areas connect to living a life of fulfillment and purpose.

Designed as both a mirror and a map, this book helps readers uncover the toxic habits, thoughts, and relationships that hold them back, giving them the tools to replace them with purpose, clarity, and forward momentum. Whether you're starting over, rebuilding, or already thriving but seeking more depth, this book is an invitation to reset and realign your life.

Back Cover Blurb:
What if the life you were meant to live was buried under everything you need to release?

In *D.E.T.O.X.*, Chef Harry Jean-Simon invites you into a powerful journey of self-discovery and spiritual renewal. Through raw storytelling, real-life lessons, and actionable strategies, Harry guides you through the five areas of detox—Spiritual, Mental, Physical, Financial, and Social—to help you uncover your true purpose and walk boldly in it.

More than a self-help book, *D.E.T.O.X.* is a movement. It's for anyone ready to clear the clutter, cut the noise, and commit to the work of healing and alignment. With every chapter, you'll feel seen, challenged, and empowered to become the person you were always created to be.

Let this be your turning point. A life of clarity, peace, and divine purpose is waiting on the other side of your detox.

Copyright Holder:
Harry Jean-Simon

TAB 2

Title:
D.E.T.O.X.

Detoxing Your Life in Five Facets to Find Your Purpose

Subtitle (Optional):
A Journey of Spiritual, Mental, Physical, Financial, and Social Healing to Rediscover Your True Self

Author Name (Your Name):
Harry Jean-Simon

Back Cover (Book Description):
Have you ever felt stuck or lost, uncertain of your next step, or unsure of your purpose? *D.E.T.O.X.: Detoxing Your Life in 5 Facets to Find Your Purpose* is more than a book—it's a transformative journey. You'll discover the path to living a purposeful and fulfilling life through the power of detoxing your spirit, mind, body, finances, and social circle.

Inspired by personal experience, Harry Jean-Simon guides you through the five stages of detoxification, helping you break free from the negative patterns holding you back. With real-life testimonies, actionable steps, and motivational wisdom, this book will empower you to shed the weight of old habits and embrace your true potential.